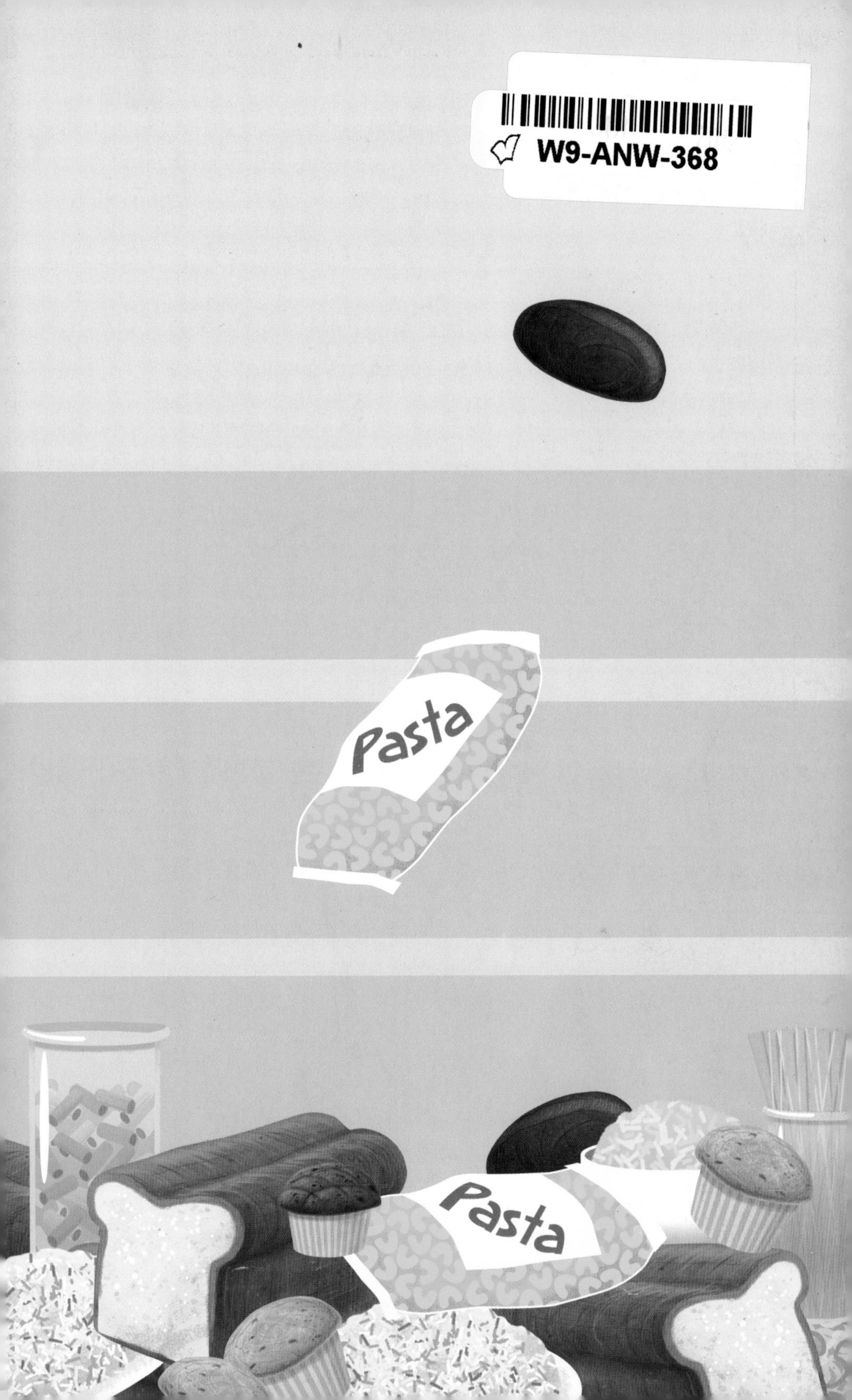
Pasta
Pasta

MyPlate and Healthy Eating

The Great Grains Group

BY MARCIE ABOFF

ILLUSTRATED BY KYLE POLING

Consultant: Amy Lusk, MS, RD, LD
Registered Dietitian
Nationwide Children's Hospital, Columbus, Ohio

CAPSTONE PRESS
a capstone imprint

First Graphics are published by Capstone Press,
151 Good Counsel Drive, P.O. Box 669, Mankato, Minnesota 56002.
www.capstonepub.com

Books published by Capstone Press are manufactured with paper
containing at least 10 percent post-consumer waste.

Library of Congress Cataloging-in-Publication Data
Aboff, Marcie.
 The great grains group / by Marcie Aboff ; illustrated by Kyle Poling.
  p. cm.—(First graphics. MyPlate and healthy eating)
 Summary: "Simple text and illustrations present MyPlate and the
grains group, the foods in this group, and examples of healthy eating
choices"—Provided by pubilsher.
 Includes bibliographical references and index.
 ISBN 978-1-4296-6088-4 (library binding)
 ISBN 978-1-4296-7161-3 (paperback)
 1. Grain—Juvenile literature. I. Poling, Kyle. II. Title. III. Series.

 SB189.A26 2012
 633.1—dc22

                        2011002445

Editorial Credits
Lori Shores, editor; Juliette Peters, designer; Nathan Gassman,
  art director; Eric Manske, production specialist

Image Credits
USDA/MyPlate.com 4 (MyPlate icon)

Serving sizes are based on recommendations for children ages 4 through 8.

Printed in the United States of America in Stevens Point, Wisconsin.
032011   006240F11

Table of Contents

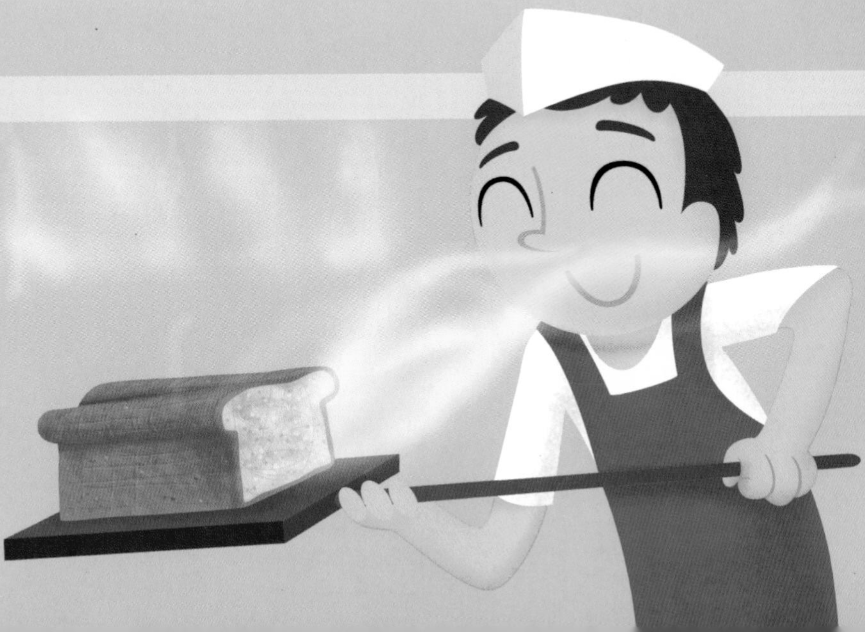

Great Grains

Eating right gives you energy to run and play.

MyPlate is a guide for healthy eating. It helps you choose the right balance of foods to stay fit and healthy.

MyPlate shows you how to create a balanced meal.
You need more food from some groups than others.

Cereal, bread, rice, and pasta are in the grains group.

Most cereal is made from wheat or oats. Some cereal is made from corn. Corn is a vegetable, but it can be used as a grain.

You can use many kinds of bread for sandwiches.

How about a multigrain bagel?

People all over the world eat rice. Brown rice has a nutty flavor.

Pasta comes in many shapes.

Popcorn is a grain too!

From Seed to Supper

All grains start out as seeds.

Farmers plant the seeds in the soil.

Sunshine and rain help seeds grow into plants.

Farmers use machines to gather the grains from the plants.

combine

After harvest, the grain is taken to a mill.

Grain Mill

At a mill, large machines crush grain into a powder called flour.

flour mills

People use flour to make breads, cereals, pasta, and other foods.

Other grains are used just as they are.

Grains have carbohydrates.
These sugars give you energy.

Sugar in grains is different
from sugar in candy. Your
body uses sugar in grains
more slowly.

Your body stores extra carbohydrate sugars in your liver and muscles.

When you need more energy, your body uses the stored sugar.

Grains have many nutrients to keep your body healthy.

Fiber helps food move through your body.

B vitamins help your body use energy.

Iron carries oxygen through your blood.

Magnesium helps build bones.
It also helps release stored energy from muscles.

Healthy Eating

At least half the grains you eat should be whole grains. Whole grains have more nutrients.

Whole grain foods are made from the entire kernel.

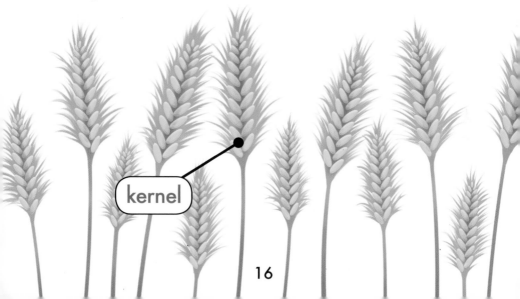

kernel

Whole grain breads and rice are whole grains.

Refined grains, such as white bread, have the bran and germ removed. This makes the grains softer, but removes many nutrients.

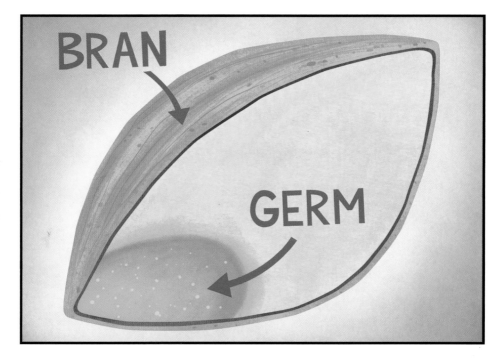

Kids need five 1-ounce servings of grains each day. Half of those servings should be whole grains.

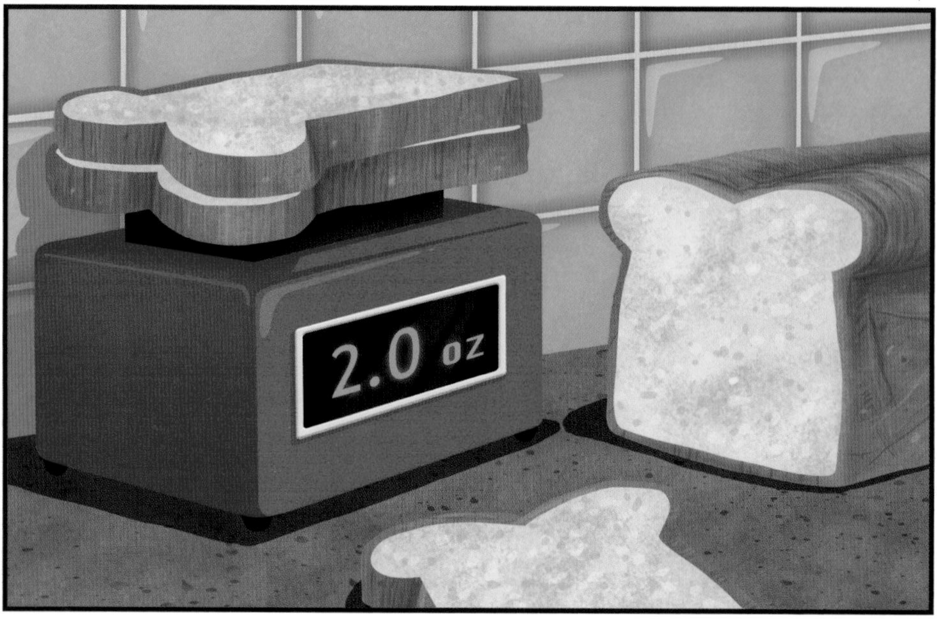
2.0 oz

It's easy to have grains with meals and snacks. One slice of bread is one serving.

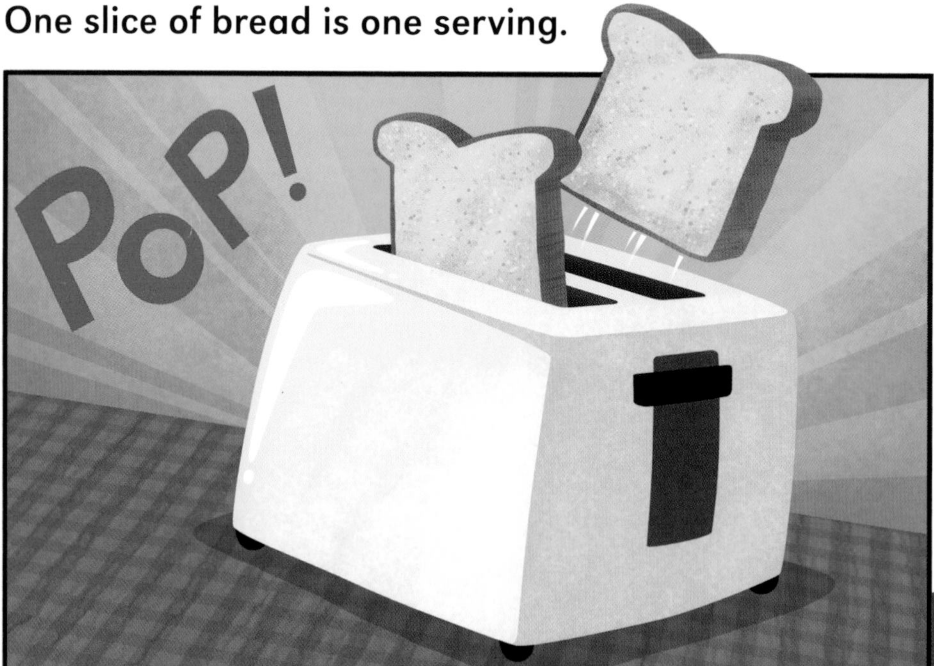
PoP!

Two small pancakes are one serving.

One cup of cereal
is another serving.

There are many great grains to try. You can try whole grain pasta.

Granola adds a tasty crunch on yogurt.

Barley can be added to many soups.

barley

No matter how you slice it,
grains are great!

Glossary

bran—the outer covering of wheat or other grains that is sifted out when flour is made

carbohydrate—a nutrient that provides energy

energy—the strength to do active things without becoming tired

fiber—a part of foods such as bread and fruit that passes through the body but is not digested

germ—the small structure at the base of a grain seed

liver—the organ that cleans blood, stores energy, and makes a fluid to help digest food

MyPlate—an illustrated guide that explains healthy eating and shows what a balanced meal should look like

nutrient—a substance needed by a living thing to stay healthy; vitamins and minerals are nutrients

oxygen—a colorless gas that people breathe; humans and animals need oxygen to live

serving—a recommended amount of food or drink

Read More

Burstein, John. *Glorious Grains.* Slim Goodbody's Nutrition Edition. New York: Crabtree Pub., 2010.

Dickmann, Nancy. *Grains.* Healthy Eating. Chicago: Heinemann Library, 2011.

Tourville, Amanda Doering. *Fuel the Body: Eating Well.* How to be Healthy! Minneapolis: Picture Window Books, 2009.

Internet Sites

FactHound offers a safe, fun way to find Internet sites related to this book. All of the sites on FactHound have been researched by our staff.

Here's all you do:

Visit *www.facthound.com*

Type in this code: 9781429660884

Super-cool stuff!

Check out projects, games and lots more at
www.capstonekids.com

Index

MyPlate and Healthy Eating

TITLES IN THIS SET:

- The Delicious Dairy Group
- The Fantastic Fruit Group
- The Great Grains Group
- Healthy Snacks, Healthy You!
- The Incredible Vegetable Group
- The Powerful Protein Group

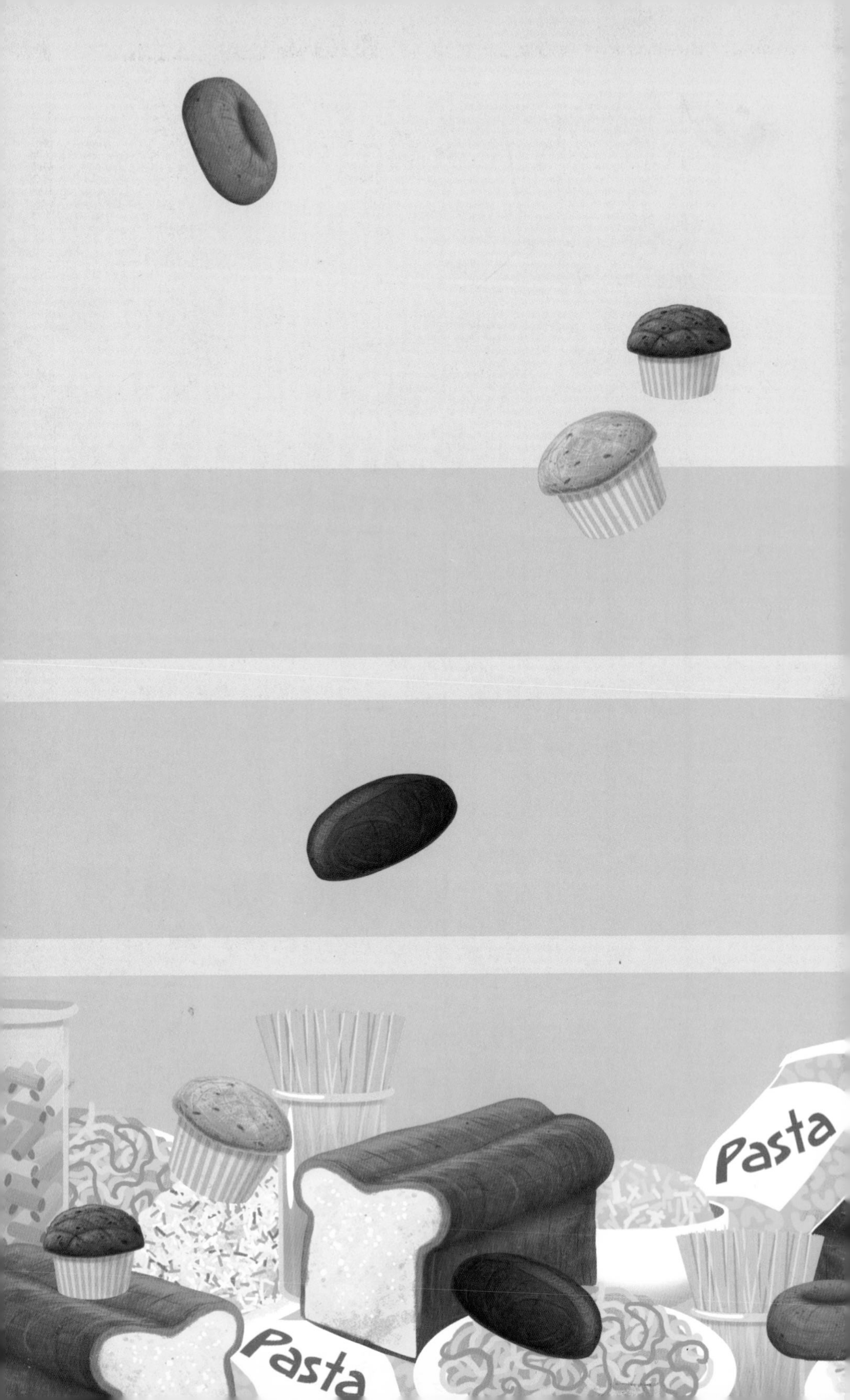
Pasta
Pasta